To Jay & Connie
Love you, Palmer
Joann

For H

First edition published in 2010 by Jo Ann Houck

EACH DAY IS A NEW DAY PUBLISHING.
10940 Southwest Barnes Road # 321
Portland, Oregon 97225

Copyright 2009

All rights reserved. No part of this book may be reproduced in any form, by photostat, microfilm, xerography, or any other means, or incorporated into any information retrieval system, electronic or mechanical, without the written permission of the copyright owner.

All inquiries should be addressed to:

EACH DAY IS A NEW DAY PUBLISHING
10940 Southwest Barnes Road # 321
Portland, Oregon 97225
http://www.eachdayisanewday.org

ISBN# 978-1-6158-598-3

Email:
palmerthepug@yahoo.com

Graphics and Design: Desiree M. Gregg
Photographer: Kim Taylor, Gene Houck
Cover: Kim Taylor

Printed in the USA
Cedar House Media
Portland, Oregon

Palmer's Broken Eyes

By

Jo Ann Houck

EACH DAY IS A NEW DAY PUBLISHING

Acknowledgements

I would like to express my heartfelt thanks and appreciation to the following people.

Kim Taylor for your beautiful photographs, your patience and your enthusiasm. You are a joy to work with. Desi Gregg for sharing your fantastic talents of design and graphics, you are a life saver and a rock. Cory Burden for sharing so graciously of your time, your knowledge and creativity getting this labor of love printed. Ellen Whyte and John Mullin for all of your encouragement, support and wonderful ideas. Phil Garfinkel for giving so generously of your time and knowledge. Sharon Peterson for bringing all of these wonderful Pugs into our lives.

My Family

Ron Houck for your amazing drawing of Palmer. David, Caleen, Gwenyth and Owen Froelich, for your support interest and love. Mason, Crystal and Bentley Houck for your love, enthusiasm, ideas, guidance and support.
To Eugene Houck otherwise known as "H" (the man of my dreams) thank you for being so giving of your creativity, time, tireless re-reads, and your touching contribution to the photographs of Palmer. This could not have happened without you.

A portion of the sales from this book will be donated to Doernbecher Children's Hospital in Portland, OR.

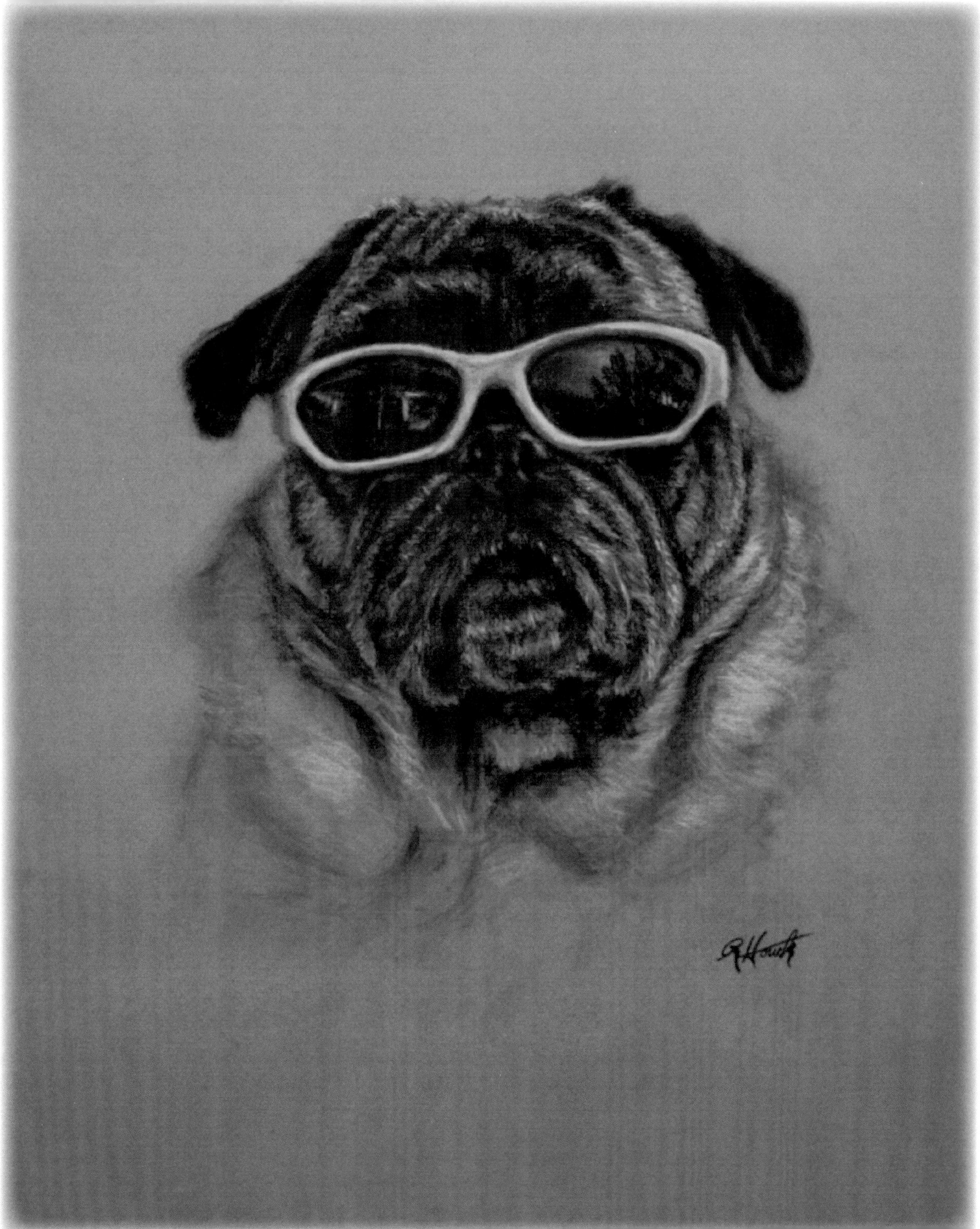

My name is Palmer. Like all Pugs, I have a flat nose and a wrinkled face. I am six years old. Because we get gray hair early in life and have lots of wrinkles, we look older than we are. I am chubby and fuzzy. My ears feel like velvet and my tail curls like a cinnamon roll. People say I am so ugly I am cute.

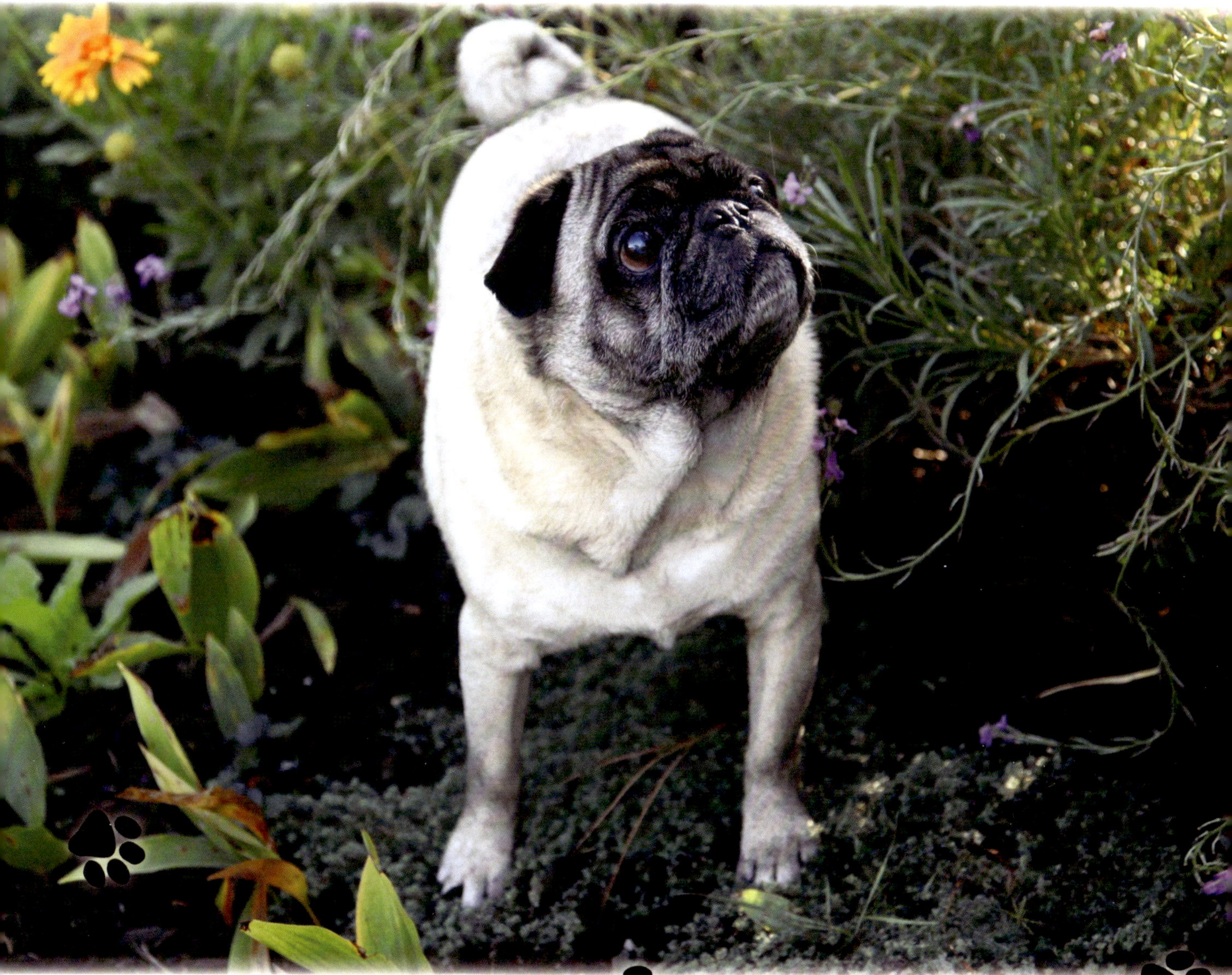

I live by a wonderful park in Oregon. My little red house sits alongside a forest. It is peaceful here.

This morning, as we do every morning, my Mom is getting me ready for my morning walk. I can hardly hold still while she puts on my backpack. I am so excited to go down to the lake to see the children feed the ducks and watch the Blue Herron sit on the rocks.

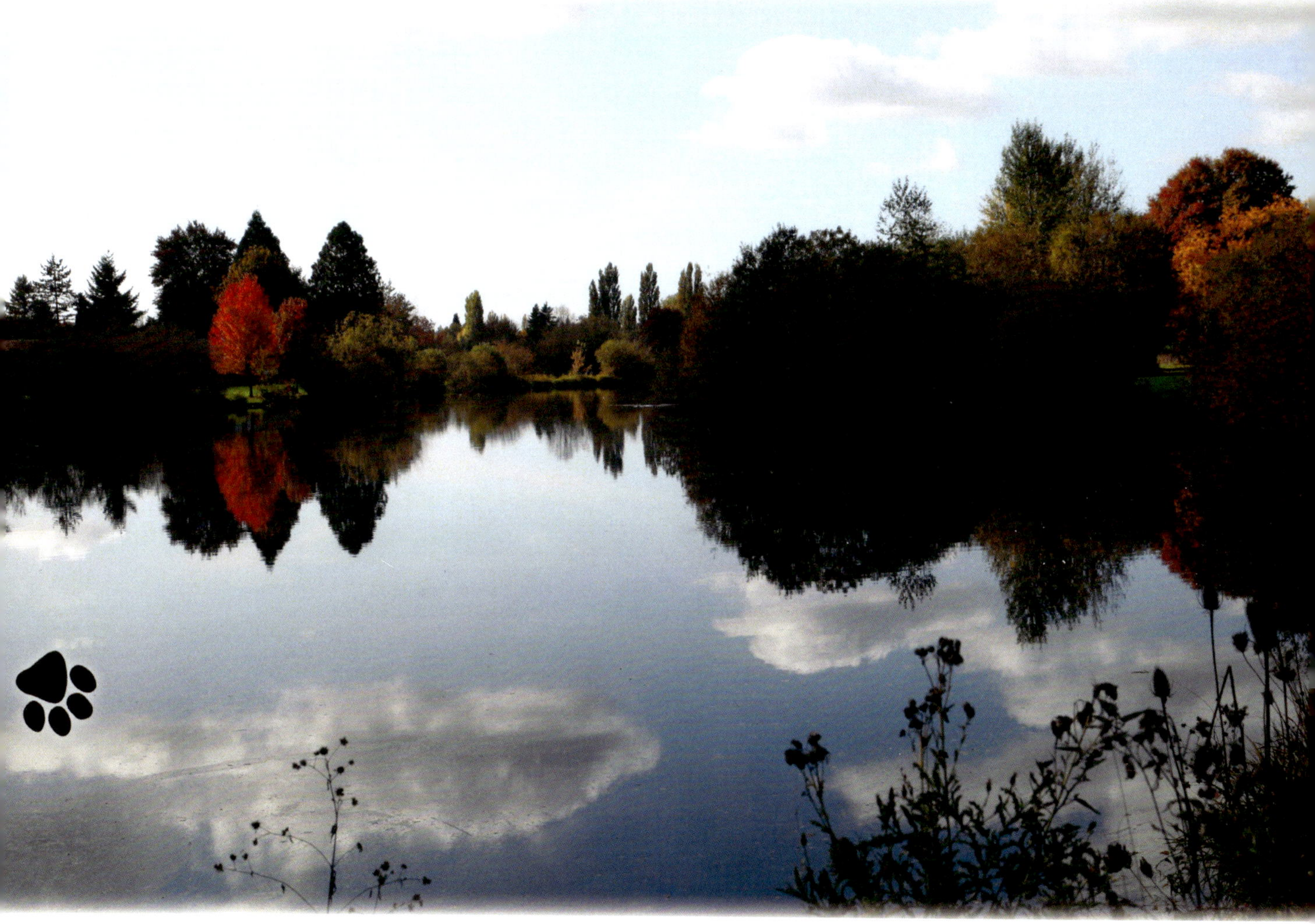

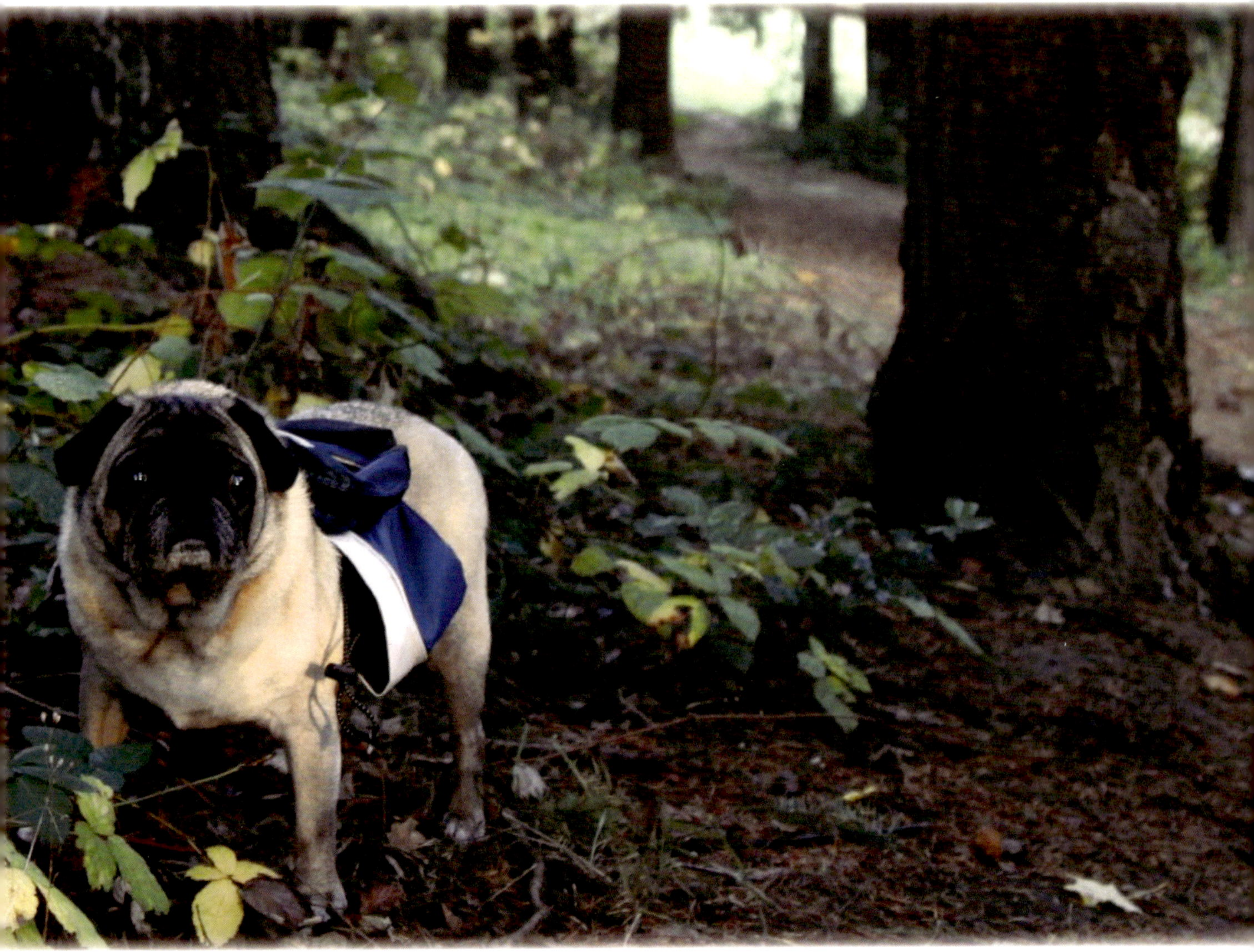

On our way home from the lake we walk through the forest. I smell the raccoons, coyotes, and other night time critters. I never run into them, though. I think that is a good thing.

I like the forest the most on hot days because the big trees make it shady and cool. The forest always feels so alive with birds in the trees, crickets in the grass, and frogs singing in the creek. It is a critter choir in the forest!

After our long walk I sit on the front porch and catch my breath. I am an old fashioned Pug who likes to sit on the porch and watch the neighbors go by. It is so quiet. It soothes a Pug's soul.

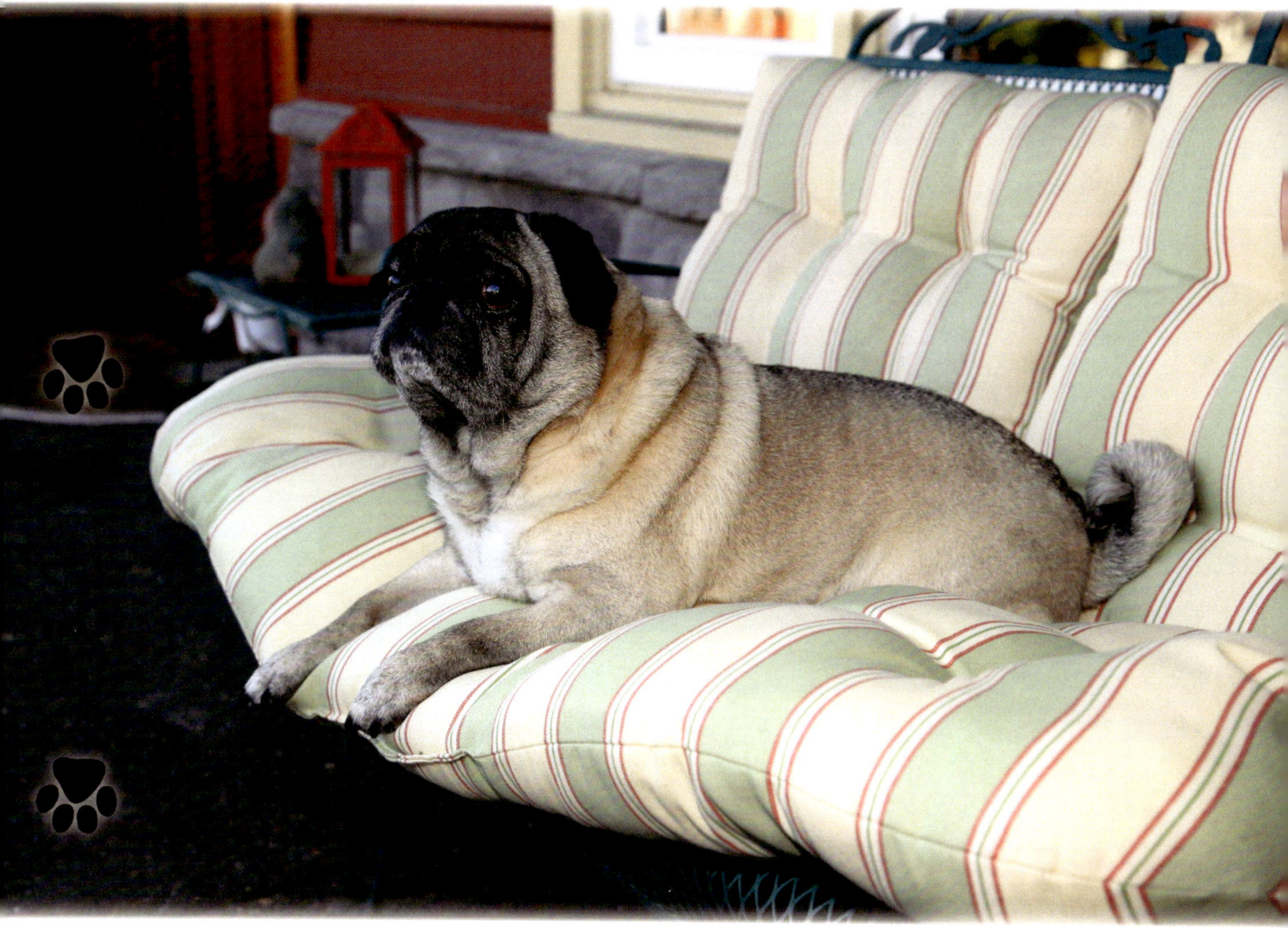

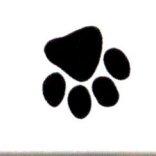

After a few minutes on the porch, I go into the back yard to see what's new. I love to sneak into the strawberry patch. I only eat a few strawberries before my Mom catches me and tells me, "Palmer, no more!"

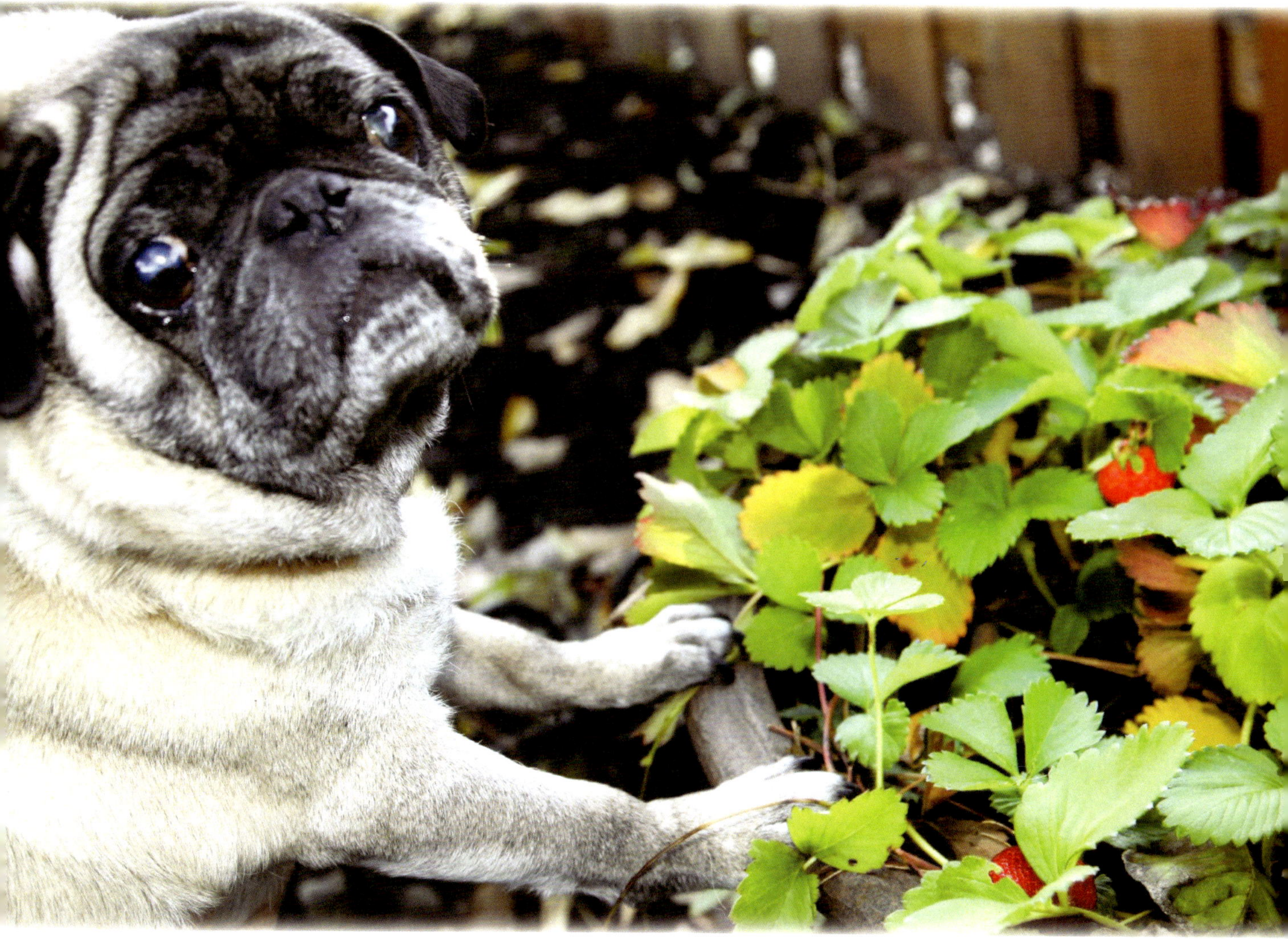

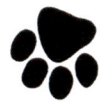

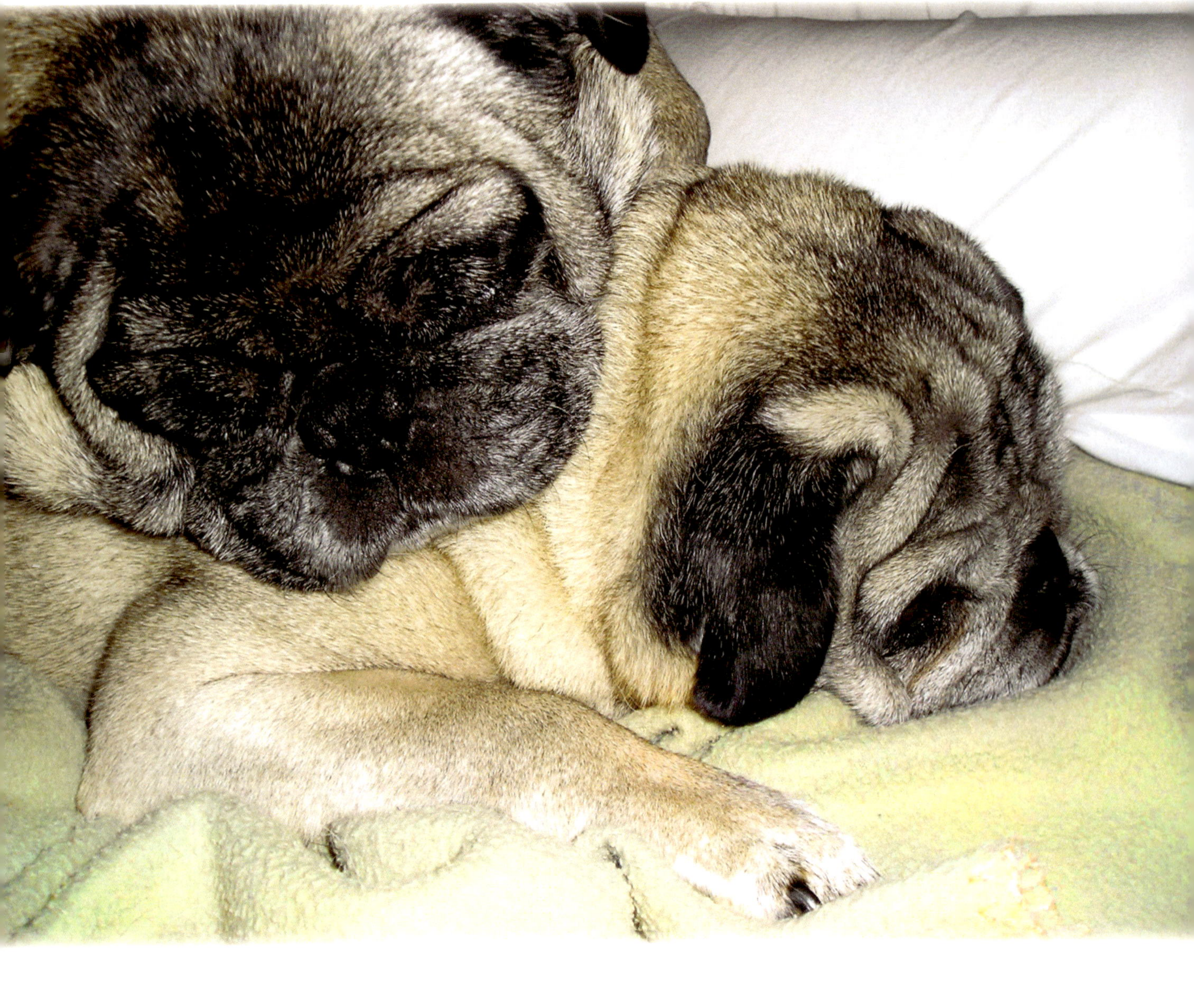

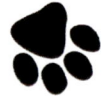

I hear the front door bell ring and I get a big Pug smile because it is my best friend Owen, who has come for a play day.

Owen is older, taller than me and not as chubby. My Mom says he is a bit of a trouble maker, because he uses chairs to climb up on the kitchen counter and dining room table. He drives Mom crazy but she still can't help loving him.

Best friends are the BEST.

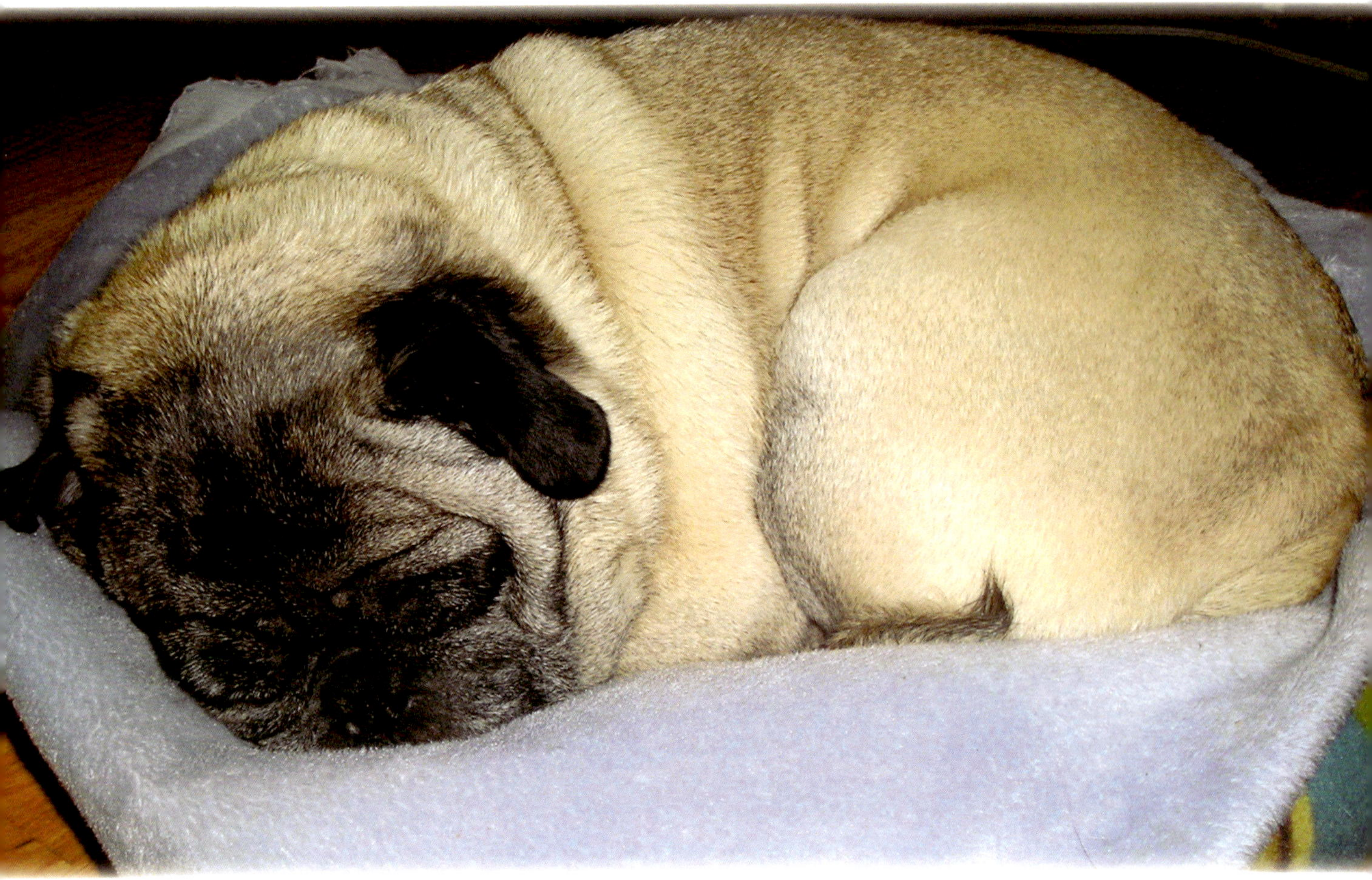

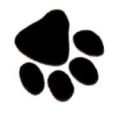

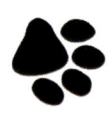

After a long hard day of play, Owen goes home. I go into the kitchen to find a big bowl of my favorite dinner. After dinner I am full and happy, so I head for my little round bed and fall fast asleep.

The next day the noisy crows wake me up earlier than I want. I do my morning snort, stretch, and open my eyes but it is so dark I can not see anything. My Mom's alarm goes off, telling me it truly is the morning. I close my eyes and open them again, but it is still dark! I don't feel any different. I think… "I must be dreaming." I close my eyes one more time and say to myself, "OK let's try this again." I open my eyes as wide as I can but again find only darkness.

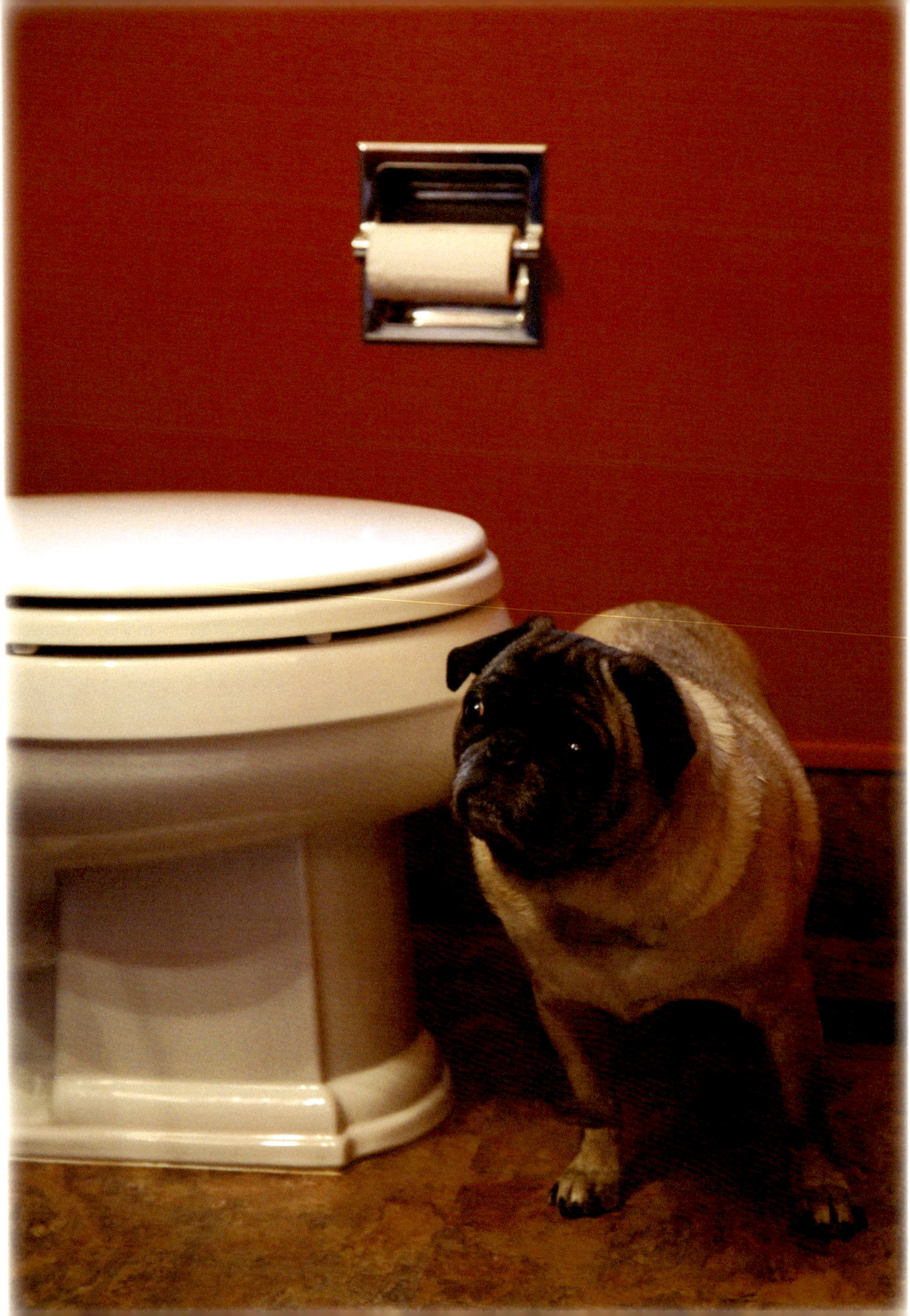

I stand up and take a few steps. As usual, I want my "breakfast" but I have no idea which way to go. I started to walk. I bump into the door, stumble over shoes and I find myself in the bathroom rather than the kitchen.

I was never afraid of the dark before, but I am now.

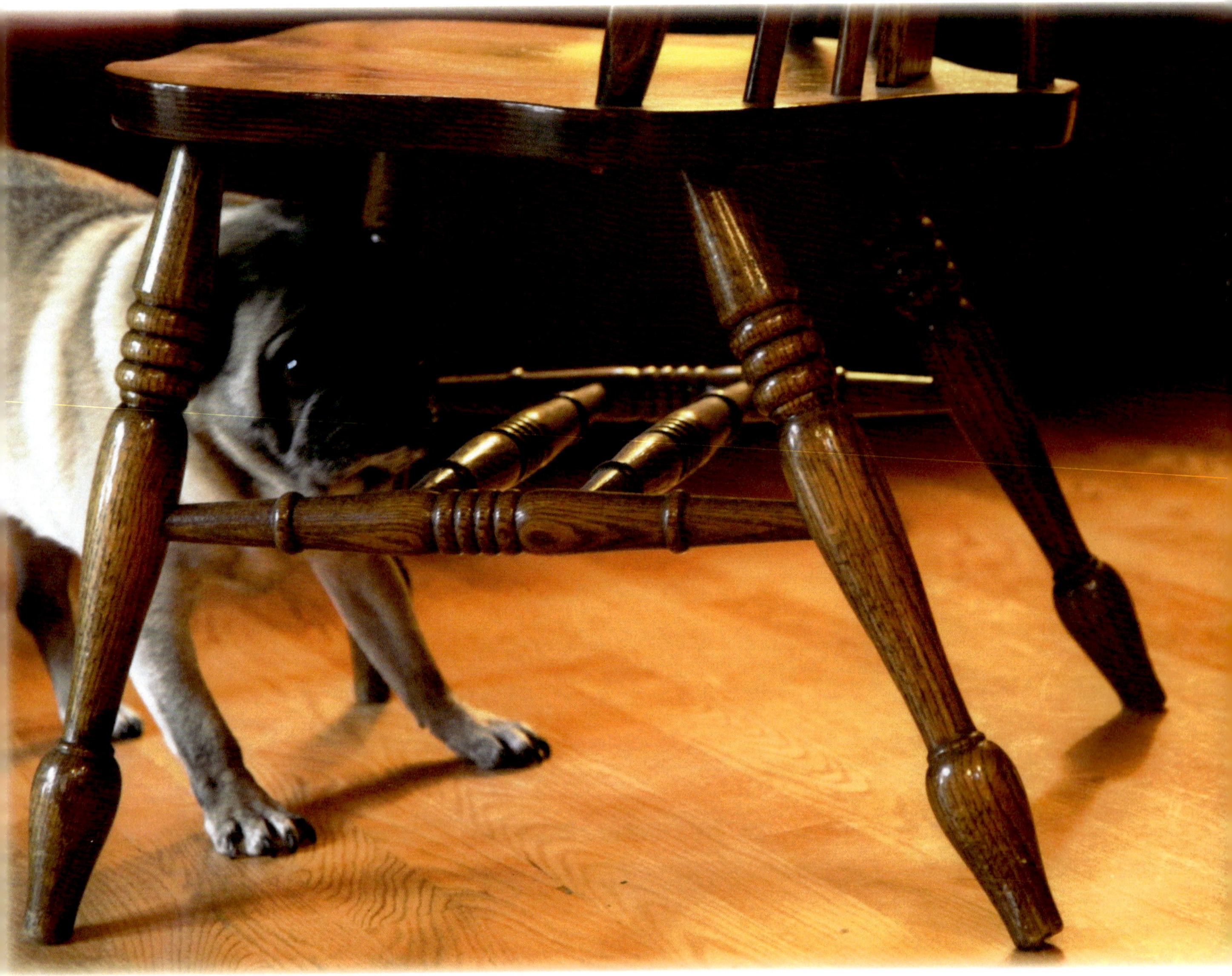

I hear My Mom put my breakfast into my bowl. She calls out: "Palmer, come get your breakfast." For those of you that don't know it, food is a HUGE part of a Pug's life. I stumble down the hall bumping into cabinets and chairs. I cannot find my bowl. My Mom says, "Palmer, come here, over here… come on Palmer, your bowl is right where it always is… what's wrong?"

"Palmer, can't you see me?", she asks. She knows I love blueberries, so Mom goes to the refrigerator and pulls out a big berry. She drops it on the floor in front of me. I hear it land. I can faintly smell it, but I can't see it and I don't find it.

Mom says, "Palmer, you really can't see. Oh Honey, Mom is taking you to the Doctor. We are going to get this figured out!"

Pugs usually don't like to go to the Doctor… but this morning I can't get into the car fast enough!

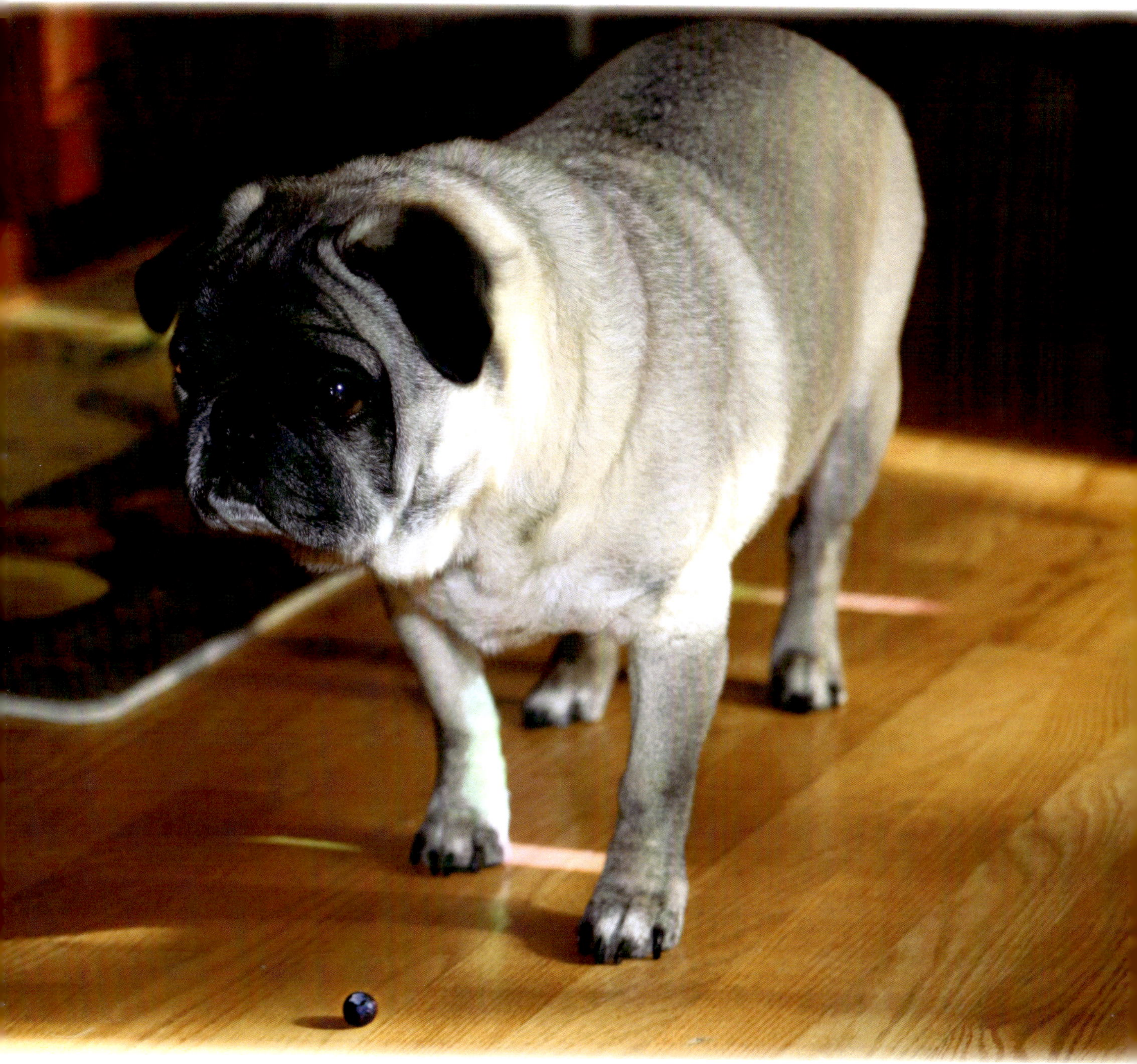

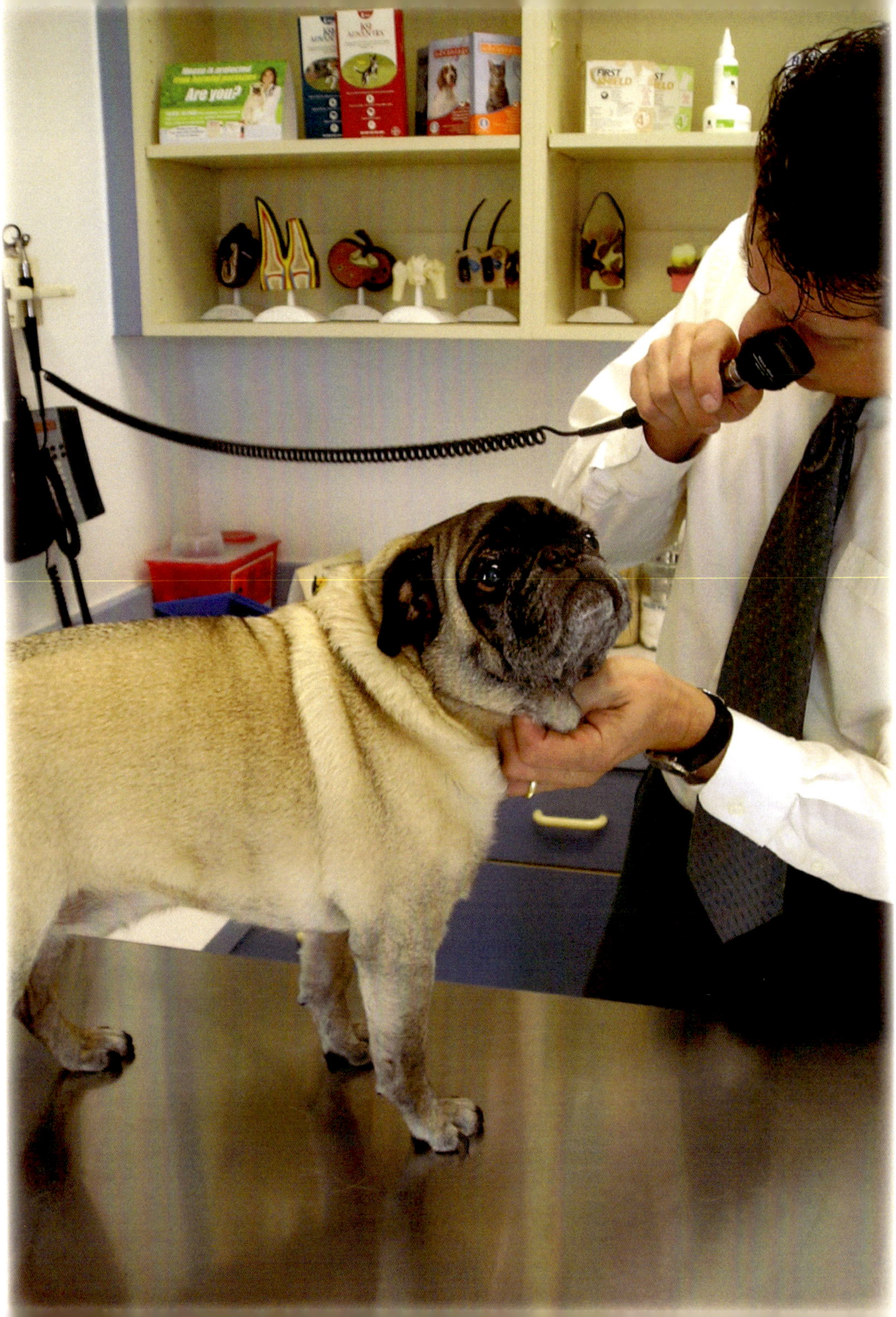
Are you?

The Doctor lifts me up and puts me up on to a high metal table. I am scared and the table makes my paws cold. The Doctor puts drops in my eyes and shines a light into them. It is not long before he turns to my Mom and says sadly, "Palmer has broken eyes."

He says, "Palmer has S.A.R.D.S." I think that must mean SUDDEN AWFUL ROTTEN DAY but he says, "It means sudden acquired retinal degeneration. I am sorry to say, I will not be able to fix Palmer's broken eyes."

We got back into the car to make a long and quiet car ride home. I cannot believe what I have just been told. Me, blind?

Back home all I can think of is, why me? I rest quietly, waiting for answers to come.

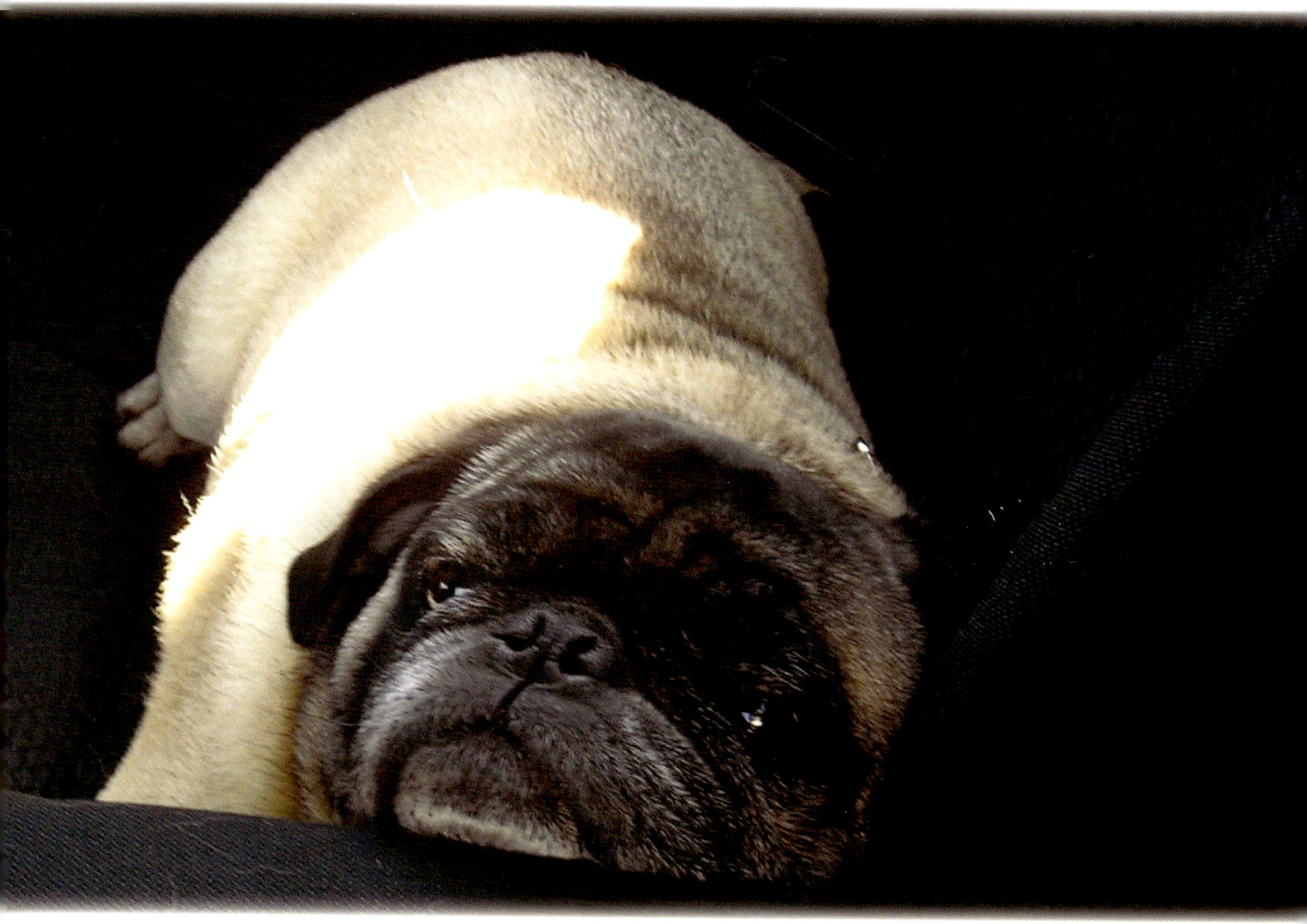

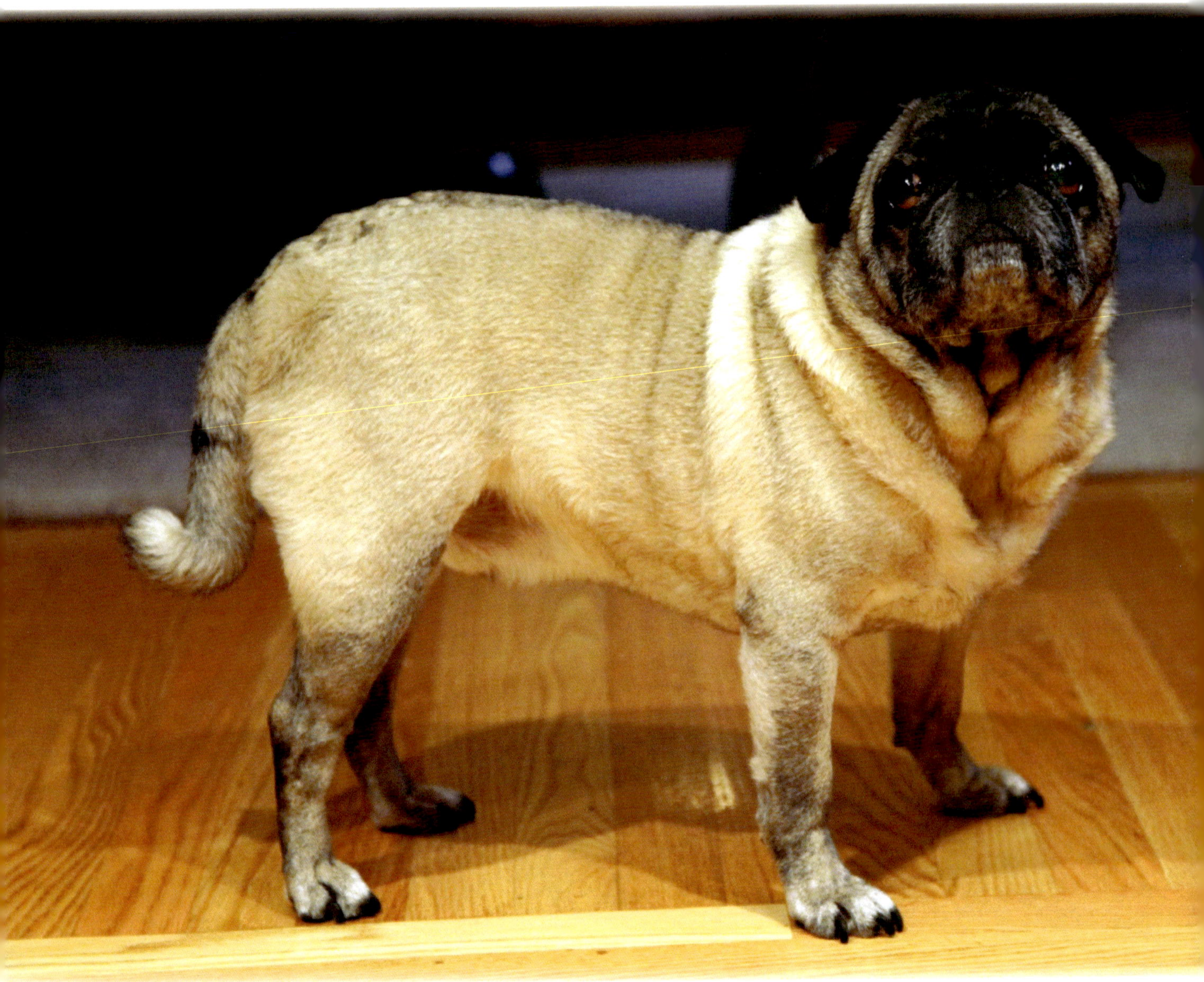

I want to believe that during bad times things can, will, and do get better. Even though I tell myself that life goes on and we can't avoid struggles, I still lose the curl in my tail.

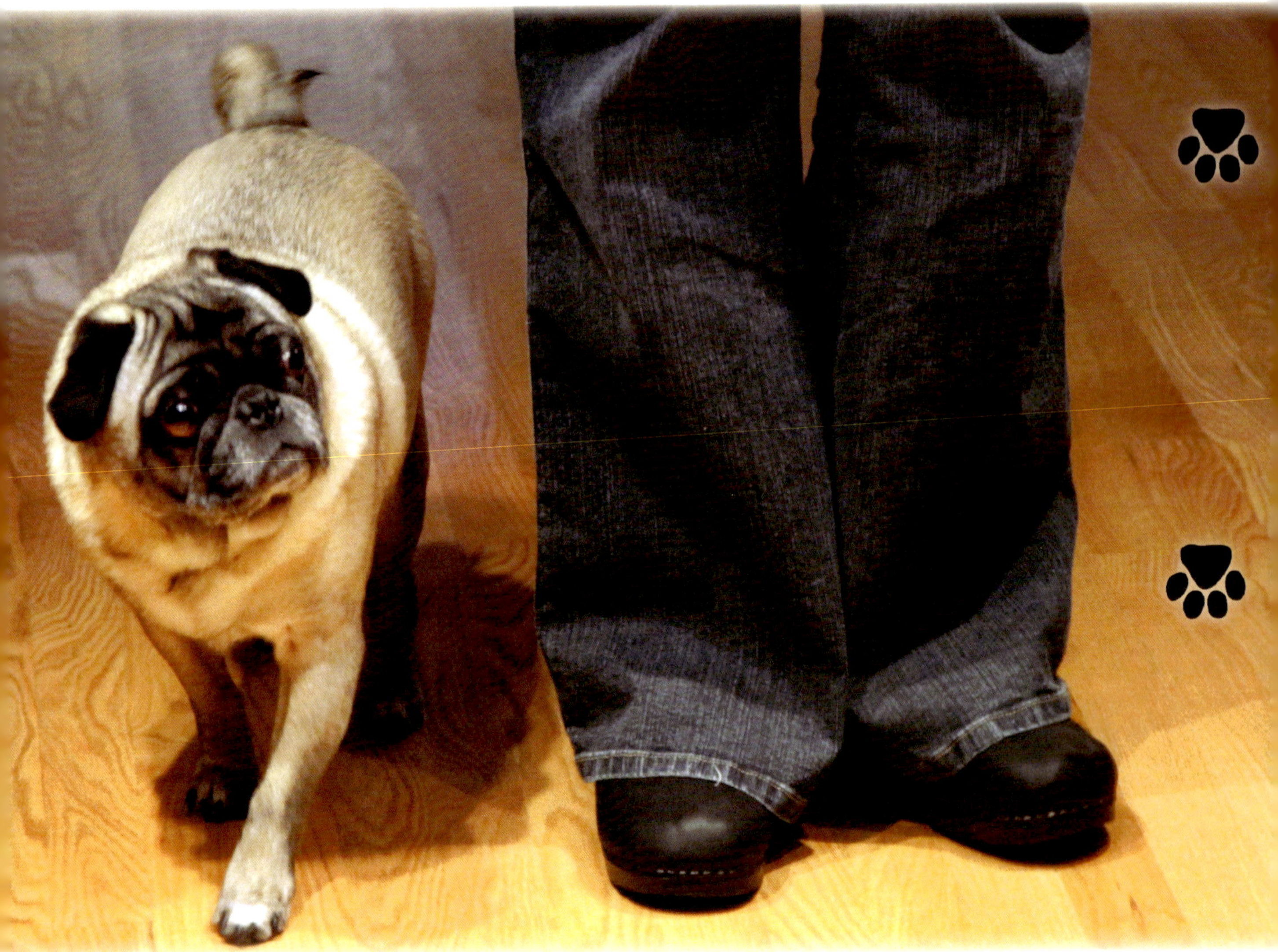

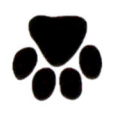

Days come and days go. I move around the house now slowly and carefully. I spend a lot of time with my Mom. I do not like to be alone. I follow her everywhere she goes. She is my map through the house. She stops, I stop. She turns, I turn. It is the beginning of learning to travel blind.

I need to be braver than I feel, more confident than I am, and as strong as I can be. Today I tell myself that my first step will be to stand up and start walking on my own. With effort, determination, courage and faith, I go in search of my new life.

I tell myself, "I can do this".

I take a deep breath and I step out into the yard.

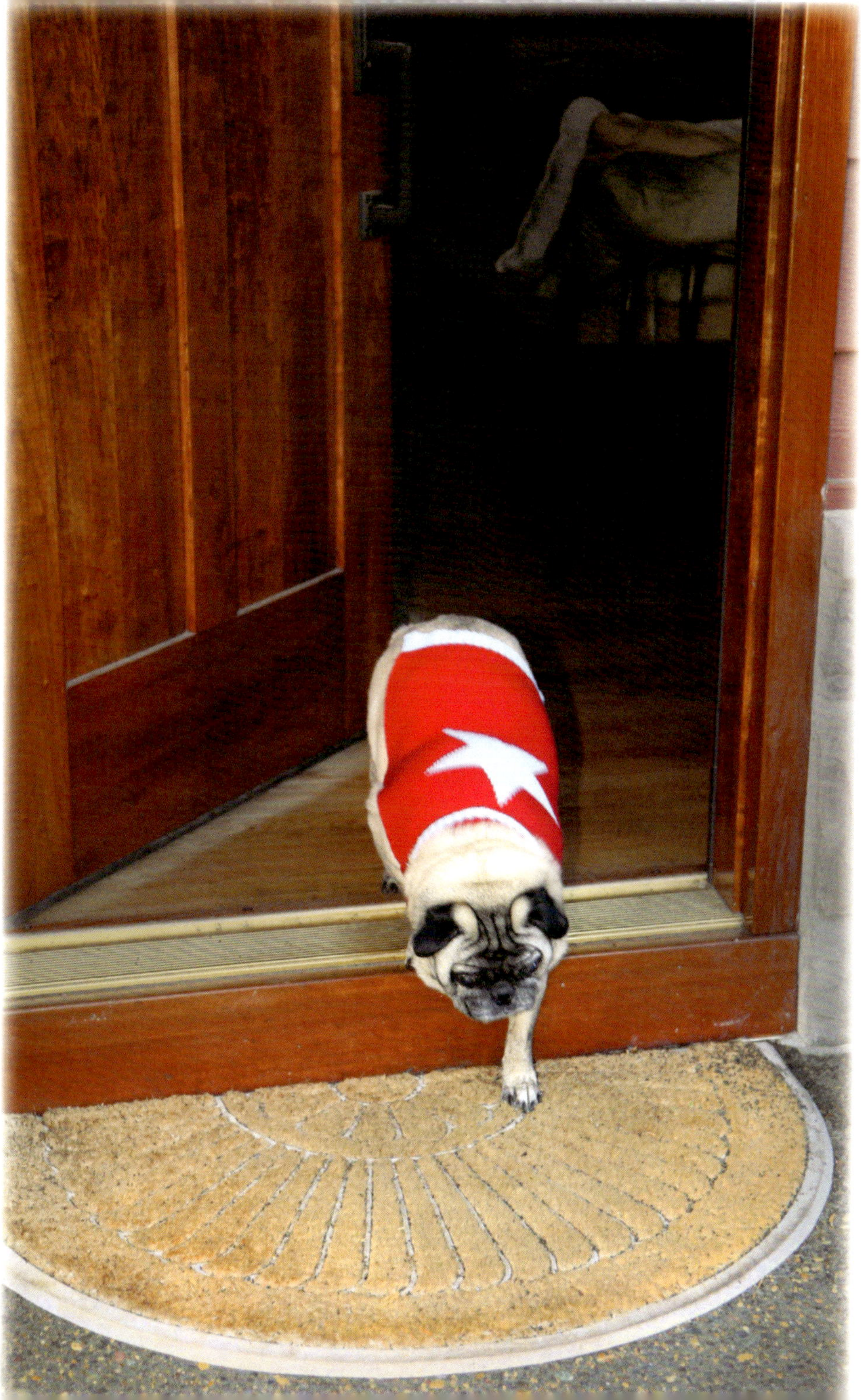

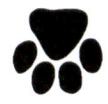

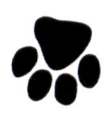

I hear my friends the squirrels running along the fence, birds in the trees, and the neighbor's sprinkler watering their yard. I love to sit here listening to everything and smelling the roses.

I am lucky to have my family and good friends. They coach me, pray for me, sit with me, and help me along the way. They all work to keep me safe. They give me many opportunities to touch, to smell, to taste, and to hear the things in my new world. I am a blessed Pug.

With their help I am slowly getting my confidence back.

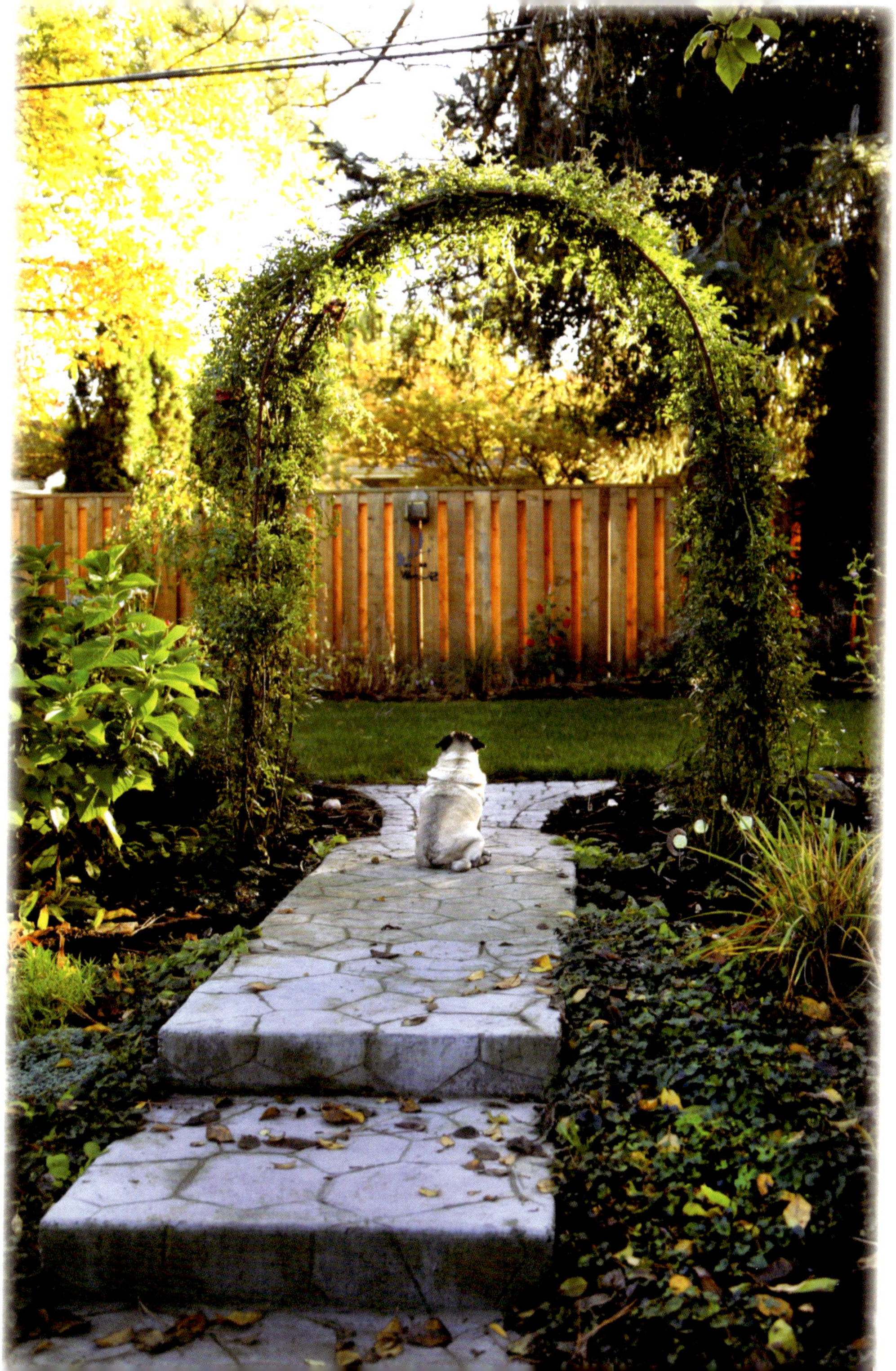

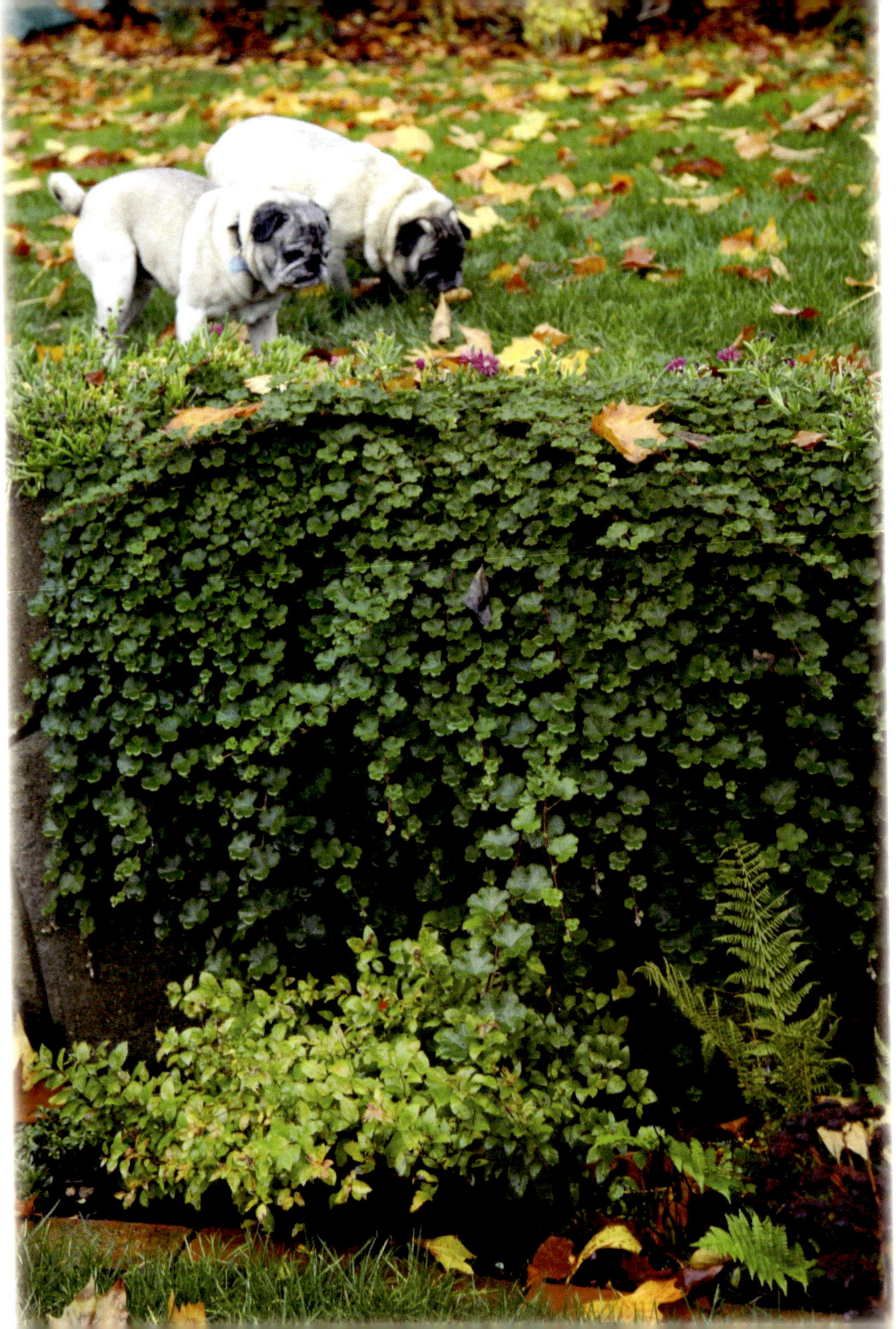

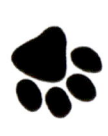

Owen comes over almost everyday. He is patient when I get lost. He protects me when I get too close to the edge of the high wall in the yard. He teaches me to be more careful.

I am learning to take adventures, trust my instincts, and live my life.

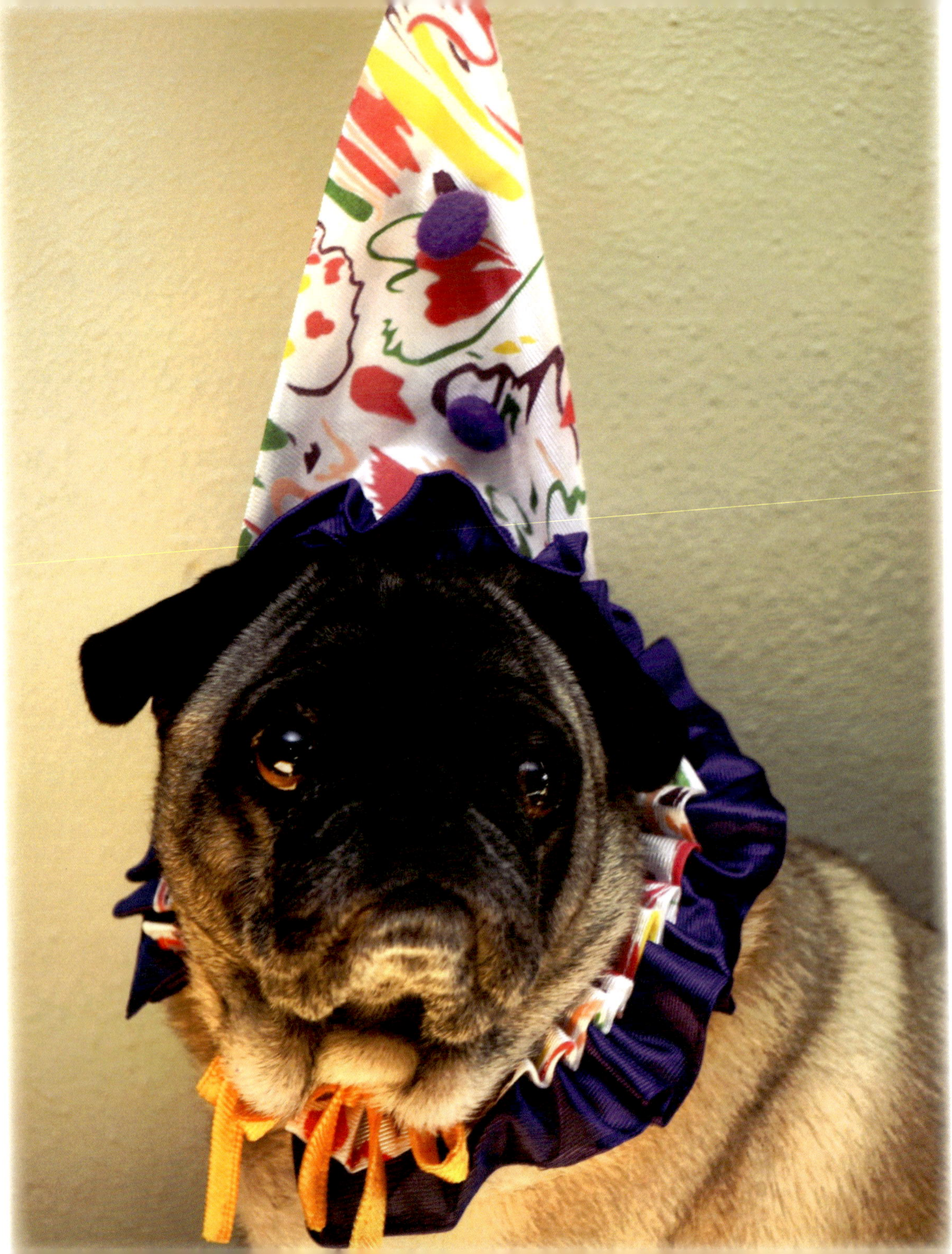

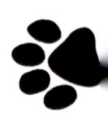

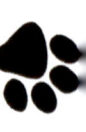

I still have sad times when we go to the park and I can not run off leash anymore. I have bad days when I fall down steps, hurt myself, or run into things… like the time I walked face first into the open dishwasher door. My pride was hurt more than my nose. I felt like a clown.

There are difficult days, days where I wish I could take off running and beat Owen in a game of fetch. I miss seeing people's faces, their smiles, and the color of the sky. I miss not being able to see where the shade is and the best spot to lie down.

I am having one of those days today so Owen came over and we are taking the day off. Mom turns on the TV so that we can watch and listen to Animal Planet.

I am learning not to be so hard on myself.

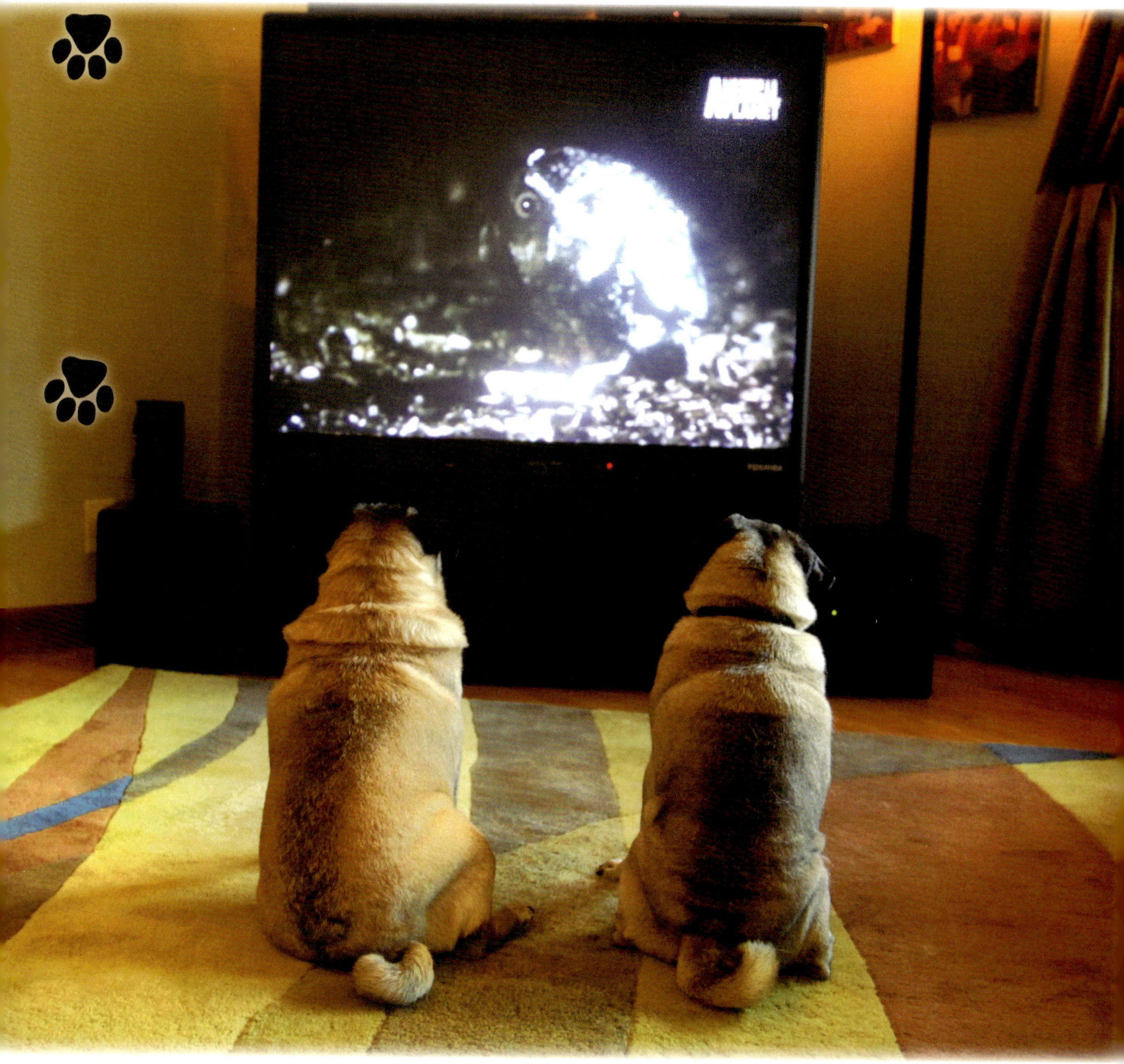

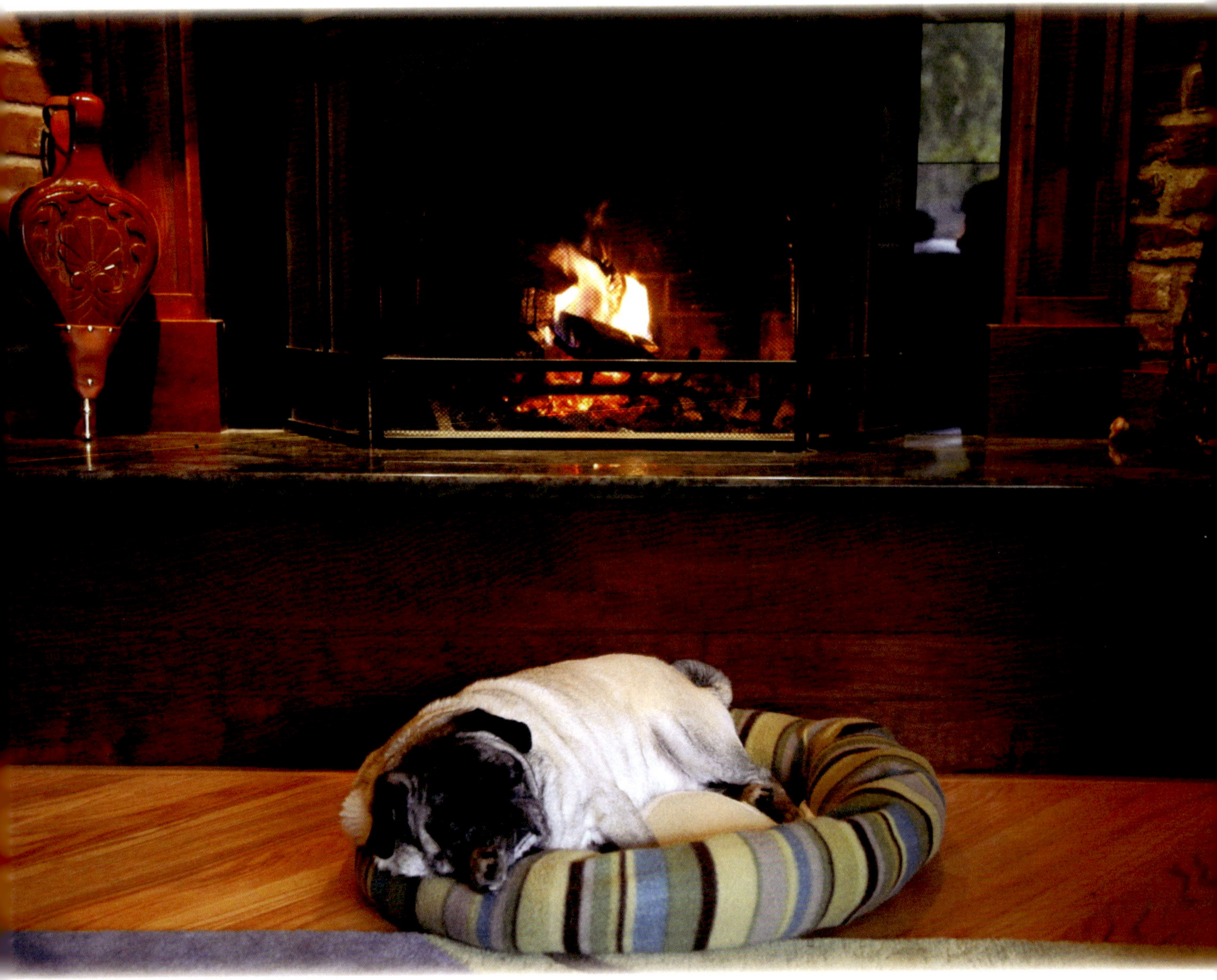

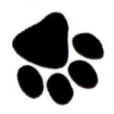

Next to listening to Animal Planet, there is nothing like a nap in front of a warm fire to improve a Pugs mood… I find my little round bed on the floor near the fireplace. I like it. I feel safe there.

When I sleep, I dream. In my dreams I can see again. I bark in quiet little barks and my legs start running. I see myself in my favorite places, like running on the beach or hiking in the snow.

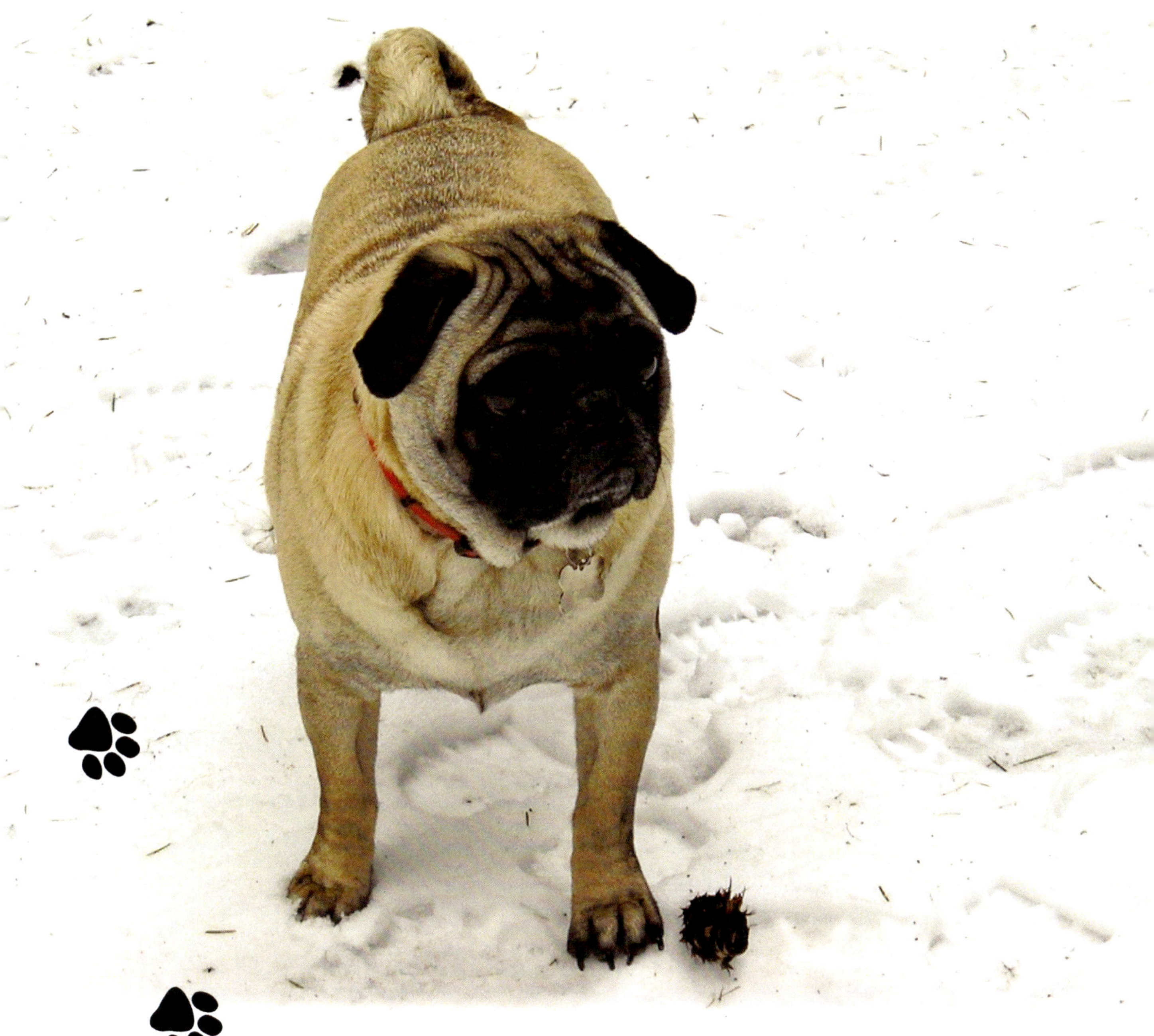

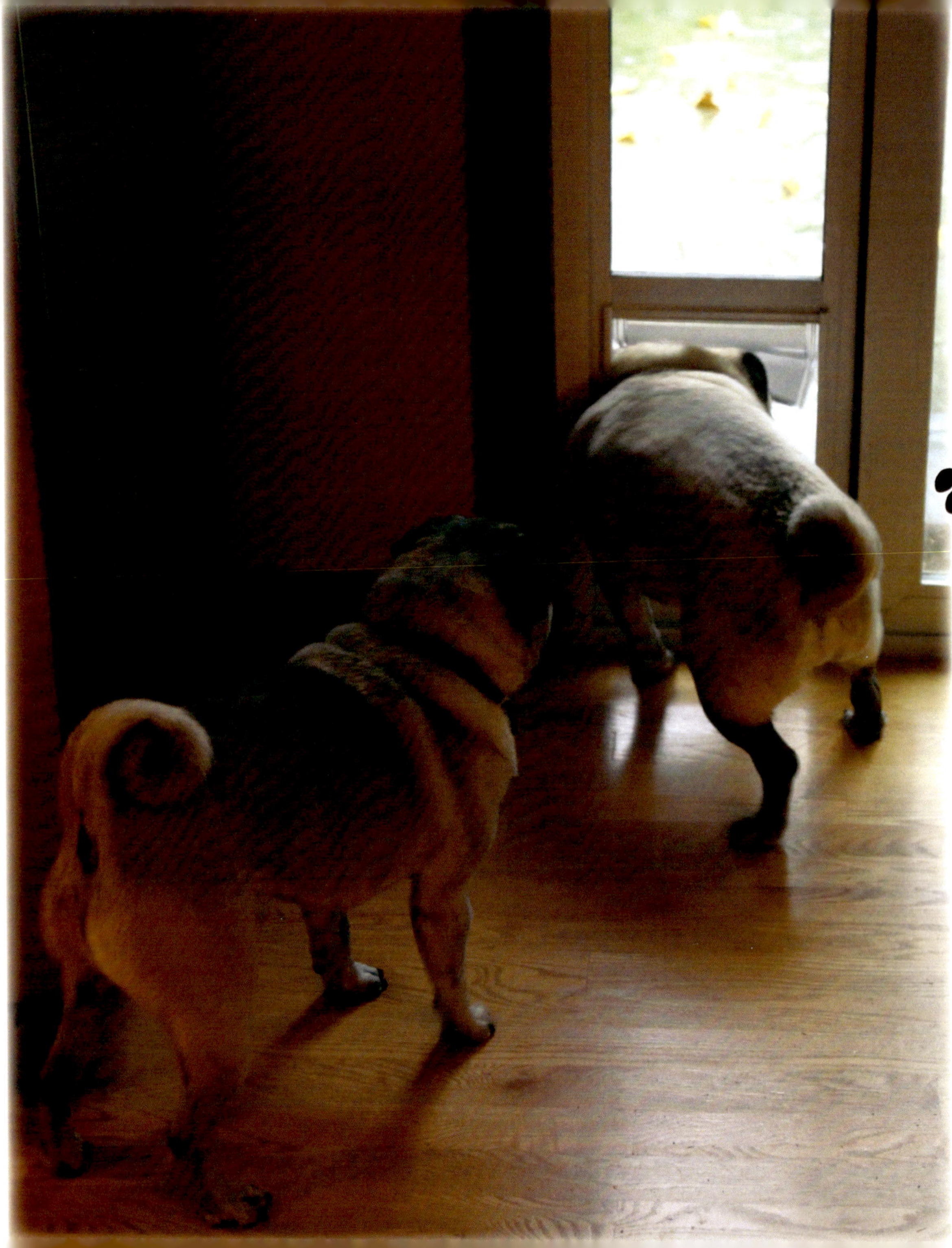

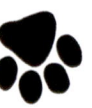

I have learned many things being blind.

I have found that even with my broken eyes, I can be a teacher. When we got a doggie door, I went through it first. I had to show Owen how to do it (more than once.)

The last thing people see when they look at me now is a blind dog. What they see is a Pug with dance in his step… a Pug who has found strength and courage.

A Pug that is smart, capable, loving, and grateful for all that he has.

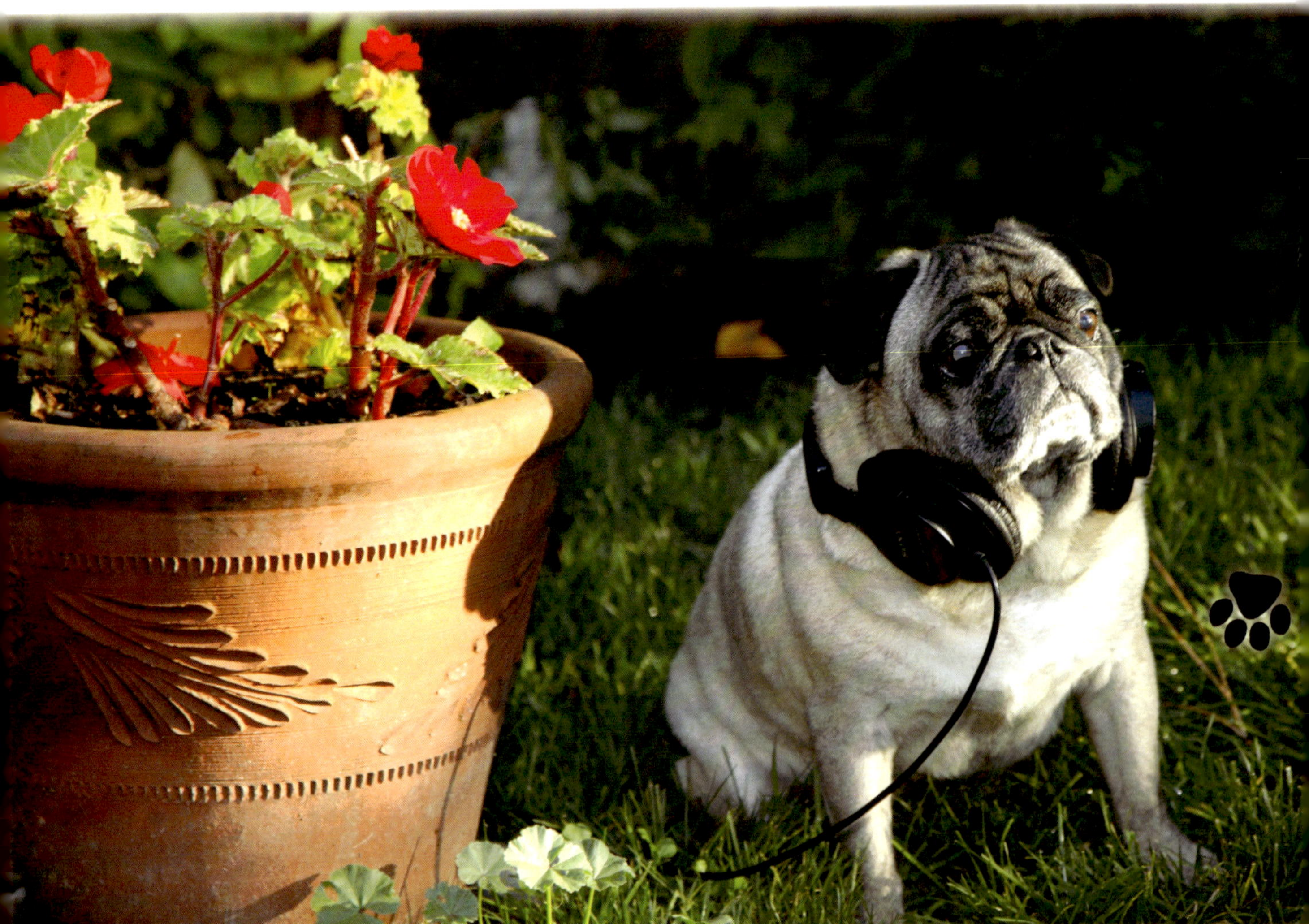

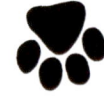

Yes, my disability has changed some things. How and where I play is different. Whom I am able to play with at times has changed but I have not lost my old friends and I have even made lots of new friends.

I have new ways to get from place to place-a new seat in the car to ride in, and my memories as we ride along.

I have favorite places to feel the wind, to listen to music, and to smell a BBQ in the distance. I have family and friends who love me just the way I am. I have grown stronger not only in spirit, but also in what I believe to be true.

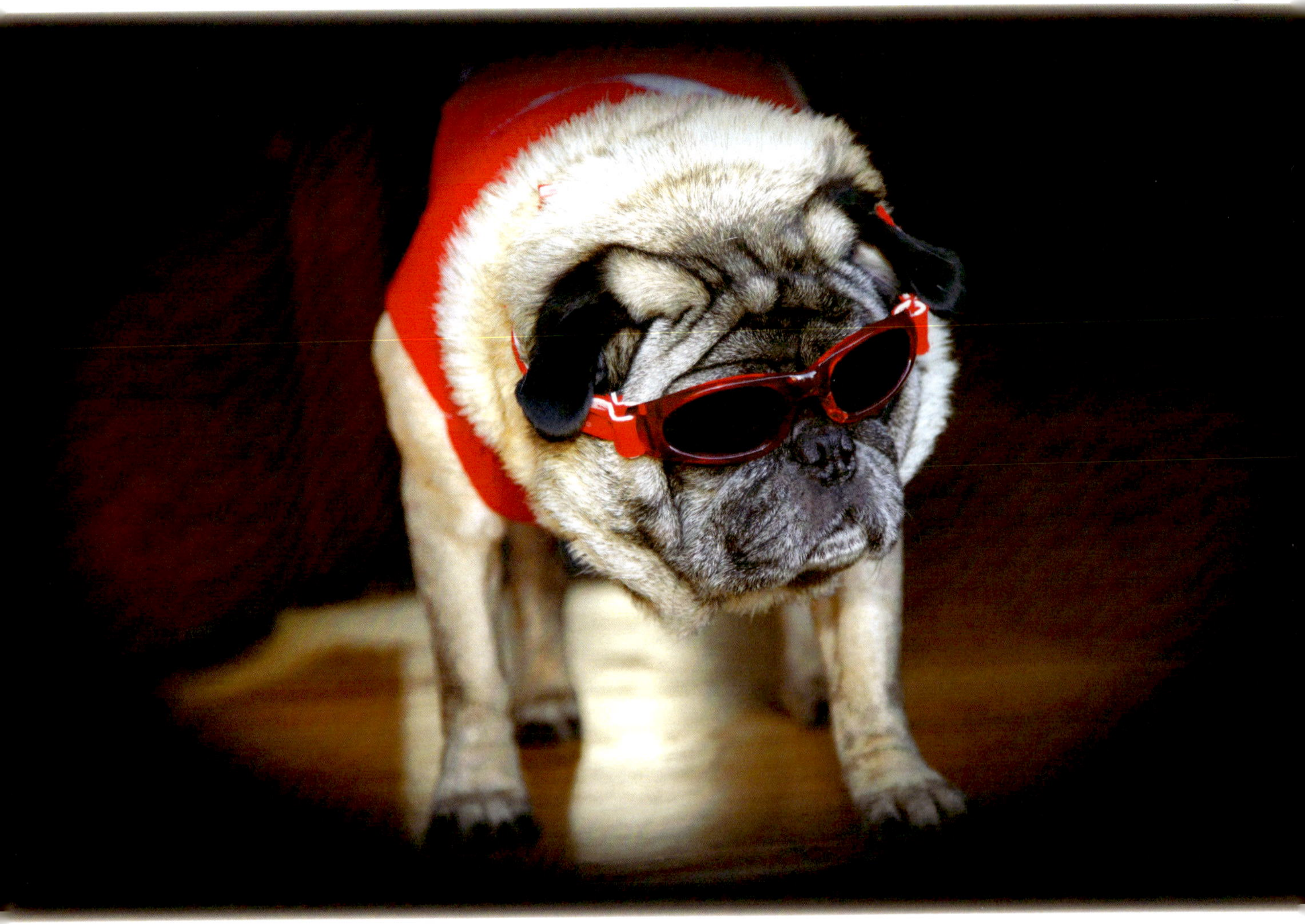

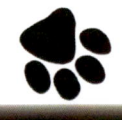

I believe that no one is blind in heaven and that one day I will no longer need to dream to see again.

I believe that
Hope is real…
Faith is real…
Trust is real…
Love is real.

What I know most of all is that I am no longer afraid of the dark.

THE END

About the Author...

Jo Ann Houck

Jo Ann has spent 30 years working for nursing services in hospitals and clinics along with 10 years as a Family Mediation Practitioner. In doing so, she has enjoyed seeing the amazing things people can do when they support each other, have faith and determination.

Palmer is the story of Jo Ann's own Pug, and the strength and character that applying that same support can bring out in our pets.

Palmer the Pug

Palmer the Pug lives in Portland, Oregon.
He spends his time with his pug friends Owen, Taxi, Bentley and Tucker.

Books in the works...

PALMER: PUGS CAN BE GRANDPARENTS TOO

PALMER: PUGSENCE ON PARENTING TEENS